Prayer

THE LANGUAGE OF THE SPIRIT

BERT M. FARIAS

A Holy Fire Ministry Publication.
Printed in the United States of America.

ISBN-13: 978-0692495384
ISBN-10: 069249538X

Library of Congress data is available for this title.

Contents

CHAPTER 1

PRAYER IS CONVERSATION WITH GOD

The highest aspiration of our lives should be to deepen our communion with God our Father. Like many of you, I fall so short of where I feel I should be in my prayer life. To stir myself, I love to read books on prayer and biographies on men of deep prayer. I also enjoy listening to audio teachings on prayer. Once my hunger is stirred my prayer life increases.

Occasionally I like to listen to an old audio teaching on conversational prayer by the late Kenneth E. Hagin. Every time I listen to this teaching, my desire to know God immediately rises within me. Dad Hagin, as so many affectionately called him, is one of two spiritual fathers I've had in my life. He is the greatest man of prayer I've ever known. In the instructional audio he not only teaches, but demonstrates how to pray in dialogue with God.

I like making this teaching available to others, but it is always with caution lest people get carried away and attempt to pray this way in the flesh. Often, even sincere people who are genuinely hungry to know God can become insensible and even weird through misunderstanding such teachings.

In this audio teaching Dad Hagin takes a few minutes to expound on how he cultivated conversational prayer with God in his own life, clearly stating that it did not happen overnight.

While warning people not to misunderstand conversational prayer and attempt to manufacture praying this way in the flesh, Dad Hagin also admonishes the people not to communicate with God religiously, but as a Father and a friend. As was his custom, he also injects humor on how a Pentecostal pastor overheard him praying this way in his room one time, and told others how *"Hagin prays the funniest prayers I've ever heard"* and how he talks to himself. Such a statement from a Pentecostal pastor reveals the ignorance of what even ministers understand of real prayer.

The year of 2013 was a year of real growth and development in both my wife and I in praying this way. It seemed to me like we received more Spirit revelation in one year than all the years of our Christian lives put together. We filled an entire journal full of notes of the enlightenment and understanding we received in prayer from the Spirit of truth. Our prayer times were marked by these heavenly communications and inspired utterances that produced joy and faith in our hearts, even in the midst of some financial challenges. Repeatedly I found myself reaching for pen and paper, and often a recorder when I couldn't write fast enough.

The first step toward praying conversationally with the Father is to be baptized in the Holy Spirit with the evidence of speaking in other tongues. It is amazing to me how many religious wars have been fought over the subject of tongues. I guess it shouldn't surprise me since it is a mighty weapon that the devil would love to dissolve entirely from the Church. Churches and Christians who have swallowed the lie that tongues are not for today, or not for them, have been dealt a severe blow from the enemy.

Isn't it interesting that the first question the apostle Paul asked the disciples at Ephesus was, "*Did you receive the Holy Spirit when you believed*" (Acts 19:1)? Paul ministered to them through the laying on of hands and the Holy Spirit came upon them and they spoke in tongues and prophesied (v 6). This is God's will for all saints.

Listen to John G. Lake's description of what praying in tongues meant to him:

"I want to talk with the utmost frankness and say to you that tongues have been to me the making of my ministry. It is that peculiar communication with God when God reveals to my soul the truth I utter to you day by day in my ministry. But that time of communication with me is mostly in the night. Many a time I climb out of bed, take my pencil and pad, and jot down the beautiful things of God, the wonderful things of God that He talks out in my spirit, reveals to my heart."

My friends, you can experience that kind of life in God if you will seek after Him. It all begins with receiving the baptism of the Holy Spirit and praying in tongues extensively. I will share how I came into the experience of that same peculiar communication with God where He talks to my spirit through the interpretation of tongues.

CHAPTER 2

PRAYER SHOULD BE ENJOYABLE

Prayer is fellowship and communion with God. If it is done right, prayer can be the most delightful and exhilarating aspect of your life. If you do not enjoy prayer then something is wrong. If you are in right standing with God and have received your spiritual prayer language of new tongues you should be enjoying daily communion with God, the Father of your spirit.

One reason many saints do not enjoy prayer is because they do not know the Word of God. Knowledge of the Word is necessary to have an effective life in prayer. Many things people pray about are either unscriptural or the Word of God already gives you the answer.

For example, one Christian man was praying about whether he should marry an unbelieving woman. Well, the Word already forbids it (2 Cor. 6:14-16), so there is no need to pray about that. Another woman, after praying and fasting to find out what God wanted her to do in ministry, supposedly heard Him tell her to pass out tracts and witness. Again, the Word already tells us that and commands us to share the gospel (Mk. 16:15).

Actually, if you think about it, feeding on the Word is a spiritual type of communion with God. You're being fed by Him as the Spirit of God unveils precious truths to your spirit. A lack of feeding yourself on the Word will result in a low grade of fellowship with God. Your faith will lose its aggressiveness and the flesh will gain the ascendancy in your life. When you neglect feeding your spirit on the Word of God the reality of divine things will grow dim and your physical senses will rule you. This downward cycle will cause you to lose vibrant faith in God and initiative in prayer. All of these things will only lead to a gradual decline in prayer and communion with God.

Another reason many professing Christians don't enjoy prayer is due to a lack of spiritual appetite. I have known some young believers who were very young in the Word, but had a ravenous appetite to know God. This alone will lead someone to seek God even if all they know how to do is pray in tongues and pour out their hearts to Him. Hunger for God is a wonderful thing and will access places in the Spirit that otherwise could not be accessed.

You can really increase your prayer life by simply using your will and desire to get in tune with God in your spirit. You can do this willingly and deliberately by meditating on the Lord and His Word, and praying in the Spirit, even while you're busy and doing other things, as well as when you're alone and quiet.

If you are hungry for God, you can have Him moving inside you so naturally, so completely, that He fills your thoughts and your very being. Communing with God "in the Spirit" can become second-nature to you and as natural and easy as breathing. God is a speaking Spirit and you are a speaking spirit, so you and God should be speaking to one another constantly.

One of the ways to speak to God is "in the Spirit" or in tongues. One of the ways God speaks to you is to pray in tongues and ask Him to enable you to interpret back to your understanding His response (1 Cor. 14:13-15). When you are experiencing the Lord this way you immediately shift to a higher level of prayer. Your ears become keen to His words, revelation, and inspired utterances. This is one of the great divine mediums of communication with God.

May you always remember to speak with reverence about this prayer language called new tongues (Mk. 16:17b). The devil has made a mockery of it through unlearned and ignorant human beings, but it is one of the greatest methods of communication with God.

I have enjoyed a number of heightened seasons of prayer in my life when my hearing became acutely sensitive to the Lord. Like many of you, it has not been nearly as consistent as I would have it be, due wholly to my own negligence and carelessness. But when you are in that place and being enriched by the communion of the Holy Spirit it is like an awakening. The reality and nearness of the Lord lingers with you all day long sometimes. And even the memory of it will whet your appetite for more.

My experience has been that the more I pray in tongues, the more internal revelation, interpretation, and inspired utterances move in me. The way I learned to pray this way was to spend extensive amounts of time praying in tongues. The more I did that the more I fine-tuned my spirit to hear.

Often I'd hear one or two words, or a phrase, and then under that unction I'd speak that out in praise or in prophecy as more words would come. When I'd sense more of an internal revelation and the counsel of the Lord moving in me I'd reach for a pen and a pad or a recorder so I wouldn't miss what He was saying. My wife Carolyn flows in the latter even more prolifically than I do.

This is the language of the Spirit. This is true communication with God our Father and the Lord Jesus Christ through the communion of the Holy Spirit. This belongs to every New Testament saint, and should be enjoyed.

CHAPTER 3

ENHANCING OUR COMMUNION WITH GOD

There's nothing that satisfies the heart like having a personal, intimate, and growing relationship with the heavenly Father and our Lord Jesus Christ through the power of the Holy Spirit. Enhancing our communion with God should be the ultimate quest of every born again believer.

Just beyond your eyesight - just beyond what you feel and know with your physical senses – just beyond the thinness of this veil of humanity is a spiritual world that is more real than the natural world. It is a realm where God works, and in which His angels minister provision, protection, and strength to us. Are you seriously aware of this invisible world?

I wonder what would happen if you started looking within your inward man. Turn off the world and everything around you, and turn to the sacred Scriptures and reflect on who God is to you. Then start turning to prayer and worshipping God, and getting quiet in your daily life and listening for a word, a phrase, and impression from Him. It may come in the way of direction or counsel from heaven to earth, or it may come in a psalm or a spiritual song of love and praise from earth to heaven. Over the years I've compiled some of these inspired psalms and songs that the Spirit of God has given me. Here's a beautiful one:

PURE PLEASURE
Not all pleasure is pure, for seasons of sin,
Thought to be pleasure, turn to misery again
But oh, of all pleasures in this earth defined
None are so pure as My Savior divine
Ecstasy fills me when to near Him I draw
Joy and delight in the heart when He calls
His voice bellows clear and I know it is Him
The conscience is quiet, cleansed of all sin
Oh purest of pleasures, to my taste 'tis too sweet
To be in Thy presence and to sit at Thy feet

These types of utterances edify you. They don't come from a song book and are not rehearsed. Rather they are Spirit-inspired and they build you up, fill you up, teach and admonish you (Eph. 5:18-19; Col. 3:16). These utterances can be spoken or sung and they should be a part of every believer's prayer life. They greatly enrich your communion with the Lord. One of my spiritual fathers, the late Kenneth E. Hagin, whom I referred to earlier, taught me these things. He told his students that he made this a regular practice in his prayer life, and a few times he'd even spoken in psalms all night to God.

Start opening the lines of communication in a different manner with God. Start believing deep down in your heart that you are a person of value and that God the Father cares about you so very much. Talk to Him as if He was present, right there where you are. Your expectation and intensity will rise when you pray and believe into the now.

When you commune with God in a concentrated and focused way like this you are creating a space in the spiritual realm where God can work and move. Too many people's prayers are not faith-filled so they are void of this reality. Being aware that God is ever present with you is one of the great secrets of cultivating rich communion with Him.

"But you, beloved, building yourselves up on your most holy faith, praying in the Holy Spirit, keep yourselves in the love of God, looking for the mercy of our Lord Jesus Christ unto eternal life" (Jude 20-21).

God calls you beloved. Let that soak in. See yourself in that high precious state of saintliness. You need a personal revelation of how dear you are to God your Father. This is where many believers falter. They labor under condemnation and being so familiar with their own weaknesses and shortcomings, but God doesn't see that. He sees your new spirit, your burning heart for Him, your yearning desire to know Him and please Him, and your eagerness to learn to commune with Him. God delights in His saints (Ps. 16:3).

Our heavenly Father tells you to be built up on your

most holy faith by praying in the Holy Spirit, thus keeping yourself in the love of God. Here, once again, we see the significance of praying in the Spirit or in other tongues. It stimulates our faith and keeps us in His love. This happens through our communion with Him.

Remember that your spirit uses your tongue to speak in the same way your mind does. The difference is that when your spirit speaks in tongues you are speaking to God. You're talking to Him, but without the limitations of your mind by which you are often unable to know what to say to God. Your spirit is the only part of you that is unlimited.

Reach out to God now further than you ever have before. Let your spirit rise to the realm where God and His angels live. Believe right now that you are capable of knowing God in a new dimension.

CHAPTER 4

HEARING GOD

I was raised in the Roman Catholic Church. When I was in the Roman Catholic Church I did not enjoy communion with God. Being raised according to the traditions of men and not according to true Biblical knowledge, everything was dead, including the poor priest himself, whom we called father. Spiritual life had not yet come into me. Then one day when I called on the name of Jesus in faith, and was gloriously converted and received that life, I was immediately reconciled to God. My first promptings were to call God Father. I was no longer an orphan. Thus began my relationship and true fellowship with God.

One of the earliest words I remember hearing in my spirit from the Father as a very young believer were these: "Like the apostle John and his brother James I use to be a son of thunder until the Lord my God tucked me under His wing, nursed me, cared for me, and patched up my wounds. Then He sent me from the nest into all the world and I became a lovebird, sharing that great love with others wherewith the Lord my God loved me first." — I wrote it down and dated it: (12/8/82)

Some people might say that this wasn't a prophecy, but they are mistaken. All prophecy is not from heaven to earth, and doesn't need to have "thus saith the Lord" attached to it. You can readily see that in the Psalms when David and others were speaking to God. Inspired utterances can be from earth to heaven, and often are, when you are speaking to God under the inspiration of the Holy Ghost. Actually, under the unction of the Spirit, prayer can be both ways, from heaven to earth and from earth to heaven.

That personal word I received might not mean much to anyone else, but it meant something to me and has and still is coming to pass in my life. There is a word of wisdom in that word.

When a person is born again he is awakened on the inside to the Spirit of truth. Then when he gets baptized into that Spirit, begins praying in tongues, and learns the Word, his spirit becomes more fine-tuned to hear the Lord. The Spirit of truth will speak whatever He hears and will show you things to come (John 16:13). What a promise!

There are many different ways God will speak to us and lead us, but the most common is by the inward witness – that velvety-like feeling on the inside, that peace, that know-so in our spirit. In the busy-ness of life, with all its' distractions and many voices, that witness is not always clear. Praying in other tongues and meditating on the Word will help sensitize that part of your being that communes with God and that inward witness will be stronger.

When Spirit-filled Christians come to me with a decision-making situation in their lives, or when they don't know what to do, I'll sometimes tell them to go pray for two hours in tongues, and when they're through, they'll usually know what to do. It really works if you'll stay out of your natural mind.

The spirit of prophecy in prayer is what makes prayer enjoyable for me – when you are praying with the help and unction of the Spirit. This is real dialogue with God when you are speaking to Him and He is speaking to you either through prophecy, revelation, or interpretation of tongues. Many cannot tell the difference yet because they are still operating strictly out of their souls (minds) and not their spirits. With exercise and use in praying in other tongues and meditating in the Word that operation can change.

I think one of the greatest experiences I've ever had in prayer was in 2002, during a prolonged season of prayer and fasting, when through the extensive use of praying in tongues, I located the channel of my inner ear and heard God speak beautiful things to me. When that season of extensive prayer was over I had 30 documents worth of notes of God's wisdom and counsel to me. Several years later I put it in a book called, "The Journal of a Journey to His Holiness". Recently one woman minister read it and told me that it was the most powerful heartfelt message she'd ever read in 28 years of ministry. I was humbled and greatly encouraged by her testimony.

Why did this dear sister speak so highly of this book? Because she was edified by its words. The words were born in God's heart and came forth under an unction of the Spirit through His interpretive processes. When you pray in tongues especially with interpretation there should be edification. If you are not being edified and built up in prayer, then something is wrong.

Most of my prayer life is not asking God for my personal needs. I've rolled the care of those needs upon Him. Now from time to time I may ask for prayer and agreement from close friends concerning a pressing situation or a need in my life or ministry, but for the most part, my prayer life consists of ministering to the Lord in worship, praise, and thanksgiving and praying in other tongues. Then from that place there is often revelation, guidance, and direction, and the inward witness of the Spirit is stronger with more assurance.

Saints, you can learn to pray this way. Yes, you can! Start praying in other tongues more. Your spirit has a voice. Your spirit has a language. It's not English, or Spanish, or French, or German, or any other language known to man. Your spirit's language is a heavenly language. It's the linguistics of the kingdom of God. And what a joy it is when your pent-up spirit has the privilege of speaking in this language! It's like a fish going from a confined aquarium into a vast limitless ocean.

CHAPTER 5

PRAYER IS HABITUAL FELLOWSHIP WITH GOD

"And Enoch walked with God; and he was not, for God took him" (Gen. 5:24).

Enoch got so close to God He took him to heaven. That verse in the Amplified Bible reads this way:

"And Enoch walked [in habitual fellowship] with God; and he was not, for God took him [home with Him]."

I love the expression, *"Enoch walked in habitual fellowship with God"*. And then, *"God took him home with Him."* Wow!

Prayer is walking with God. It is habitual fellowship with God. You can walk so close to God that you feel like you're in heaven. It is cultivating a receptivity and sensitivity to His presence that will move you toward this richness of communion with Him.

One day a man asked the Lord this question: "What is it you desire, Lord? What is on Your heart?

The Lord responded: *"I enjoy it when My people just like being with Me, not asking anything of Me, just enjoying Me, for it is then that we enter into true communion and fellowship. This is my great desire;*

fellowship – to be with My people, that My people would enjoy Me for just being Me. This is true worship."

I weep when I read that for it touches me deeply.

Many people only pray when there is a crisis. "Help!" they cry out. And the Lord does help them.

Others pray like they are taking an order at a restaurant. "I'll have a hamburger and a small order of fries." And the Lord will deliver.

Others pray as if they are on a business trip. "There's a job to be done." Yes, there is, but it's in Him that it will get done.

Yet others will use praise and worship as a means of manipulating an answer from the Lord. "Like if I just praise Him enough He will send the answer." And in spite of us, He often will.

When you think about it, though, how many really have learned to walk with the Lord as a close friend? This is the kind of walk that is really valued by the Lord.

Loneliness and sorrow fill the heart of the Lord for those of His children who treat what He's done for them with so little respect and are caught up in this world's pleasures.

Think for a moment about creation. God called everything He created good, especially man (Gen. 1). God knew you before you were born.

"Before I formed you in your mother's womb I knew you; before you were born I sanctified you..." (Jer. 1:5)

I love Psalm 139 for it contains God's perfect knowledge of man.

"I will praise you, for I am fearfully and wonderfully made..." (v 14)

The psalmist seems to pour through the knowledge God has of him in these verses, and then from a heart enlightened to God's beauty, he exults forth toward the end of his reflection with this phrase:

"How precious also are Your thoughts to me, O God! How great is the sum of them!"

Have you ever thought of your own uniqueness and how God fashioned you? He took time and effort in the design of every human being, and He loves them equally well. Your likes and dislikes are a product of His imagination. He thought you up.

My wife Carolyn loves roller coasters. I'm afraid of them! The higher they go, the faster they roll, the more Carolyn loves them. God put that "like" in her. I made the mistake one time of going on one with her and I almost died. I'm ashamed to admit it, but I was holding on to her leg all the way down. It's funny now but it wasn't then.

Before God ever made the earth He thought of how He would shape our personalities, our circumstances, our time of birth and purpose in this life for all human beings who have ever lived.

What about those born into difficult circumstances? God put enough ability and strength in them to overcome every difficulty as they seek Him.

What about babies and innocent children who die or are killed? They're with Jesus! And He will display the exceeding riches of His grace and His kindness to them in the ages to come (Eph. 2:7).

God is fair and just, and none of us will be able to find fault with Him on judgment day.

Your prayer life and fellowship with God will change when you get your perception of Him right. Your prayer life and fellowship with God will change when you get *His* perception of you right. How do you see Him? And how do you see yourself in relation to Him?

You are His beloved. He's waiting for you. He enjoys you. You are your Father's child. You are your Savior's prized and purchased possession. He longs for your friendship.

Grace to learn to walk with Him habitually abounds to you now. Selah.

CHAPTER 6

KNOWING GOD'S TRUE CHARACTER

I've stated repeatedly that prayer is communication with God. It's not one way – not a monologue, but a dialogue. It takes His voice, His presence, and intimacy with the Lord to really experience Him. This is the reason prayer is boring to most Christians – it's void of the reality of His presence and voice. Christians must experience God to enjoy Him.

If I met you on the street and just said, "Hello, how are you?" and went my way, would you say that I experienced you? But if instead, I sat down with you and told you how much I loved and appreciated you, and how precious and valuable you were to me, and you reciprocated the same way back to me, could you then better say that we experienced one another?

You see, prayer is not just what you say, but what you hear. What are you hearing in prayer? "You dirty backslider, why are you always sinning? Why don't you get your life cleaned up and start obeying Me?" or some version of that, is what some people only hear. This is one of the biggest reasons many Christians do not experience or enjoy God. They don't see Him as He is. They don't know His character. They are guilt-ridden and always accusing themselves.

"My little children, let us not love in word or in tongue, but in deed and in truth. And by this we know that we are of the truth, and shall assure our hearts before Him. For if our heart condemns us, God is greater than our heart, and knows all things. Beloved, if our heart does not condemn us, we have confidence toward God. And whatever we ask we receive from Him, because we keep His commandments and do those things that are pleasing in His sight" (1 John 3:18-22).

Loving in action, and not in word only, produces assurance in the face of our Father. Now, if you are not living right before God, then your own heart will condemn you. You certainly cannot enjoy God living a life that you know is displeasing to Him. You will have no confidence in prayer. But God is greater than our hearts and is always working on our behalf to bring us back into fellowship with Him. He is for us, and not against us. He will never keep us from His presence by pointing out our sins and shortcomings.

If you had an employer who was always reprimanding you and pointing out your mistakes only, would you want to work for him? I think not. God our Father does correct us, as all good earthly fathers do, but that is not all He does. Do you see God as only an employer that you go to work for? If so, that is as far as your fellowship will go. At the same time, if you only see Him as a pie in the sky sort of God – a Santa Claus, a vending machine who beckons at your every whim and whine, then you are still very limited in your image of Him.

Knowing God is a lifelong process. We are all at different stages of growth, and God treats us according to our level of maturity. Again, a good earthly father has that much sense. You don't treat your 3 year old son like you do your 16 year old. Our heavenly Father is the same way.

I want to help you develop in your hearing so that your communion with God will not be a monologue only. What do you hear in prayer? How do you hear? How do you see God? How do you see yourself in relation to Him? It takes a real knowledge of the Word to understand God's true manifold character and beauty, and how He sees humanity, especially His own children.

For example, one day I read a verse, Mark 16:9, and was arrested. I was intrigued by the fact that Jesus' first post-resurrection appearance was to a woman who used to have 7 devils. The Holy Spirit highlighted this verse to me and I stopped to meditate on it. The words spoke to me deeply about the other-worldliness and beauty of our God, and it made me want to love Him and know Him more.

In the greatest moment ever in human history Jesus did not seek out the king, or governor, or some magistrate or important figure to tell the news of His resurrection to. He went to a former lowly woman of ill repute who probably once lived the gutter life on the streets. Most mere men would never go that route and visit such a one after a marked moment in history of the most glorious resurrection. Jesus' visit with this woman is just one example of a multitude of others demonstrating just one facet of God's character.

The magnificent attributes of God should encourage love, faith, prayer, and praise in us. Most sincere Christians love God, but they are not too crazy about themselves. Again, the Word will help us here in seeing ourselves in Christ, no longer as sinners, but as new creations, and His beloved sons and daughters. The problem with many of us is in the area of unforgiveness; not only forgiving others, but forgiving ourselves. Many of us remember our sins of yesterday, which we repented of, that God has long forgotten. Too many Christians beat themselves over the head for sins of the past. Forgetting the past is one of the great secrets of living free and being able to draw close to God.

When a true believer sins there are two voices that will immediately speak to him. One is the voice of accusation, which breeds condemnation. The other is the voice of correction, which fosters conviction. Knowing the difference will allow you to jump a major hurdle that keeps many believers out of close fellowship with God. When Satan accuses the believer it crushes your motivation to try again. But when the Holy Spirit convicts the believer it is gentle, peaceable, and easy to be received and motivates you to keep moving forward with God.

Obedience is what will give your heart assurance before God. So once you've received God's mercy and forgiveness, go on and receive His grace that empowers you to obey God.

"Let us therefore come boldly to the throne of grace, that we may obtain mercy and find grace to help in time of need" (Heb. 4:16).

Mercy is for our sins and failures. Grace is to help us and empower us in our weaknesses. You see, God is always working for us so we can come boldly and confidently before Him and enjoy His presence.

CHAPTER 7

SEEING GOD

"But Martha was distracted with much serving, and she approached Him and said, 'Lord, do You not care that my sister has left me to serve alone? Therefore tell her to help me.' And Jesus answered and said to her, 'Martha, Martha, you are worried and troubled about many things. But one thing is needed, and Mary has chosen that good part, which will not be taken away from her'" (Lk. 10:40-42).

Inspect your life and soul and find out what things pull you out of the Spirit and from a place of rest. Watch for things that take you out of a love walk and bring offense or anxiety.

It is as men live that they pray. How you live affects the way you pray, and vice versa; how you pray affects the way you live. Some Christians want their prayers answered, but they're not that interested in having a real relationship with the Lord. Frankly, at this stage of my life and spiritual growth that is a hard one to wrap my mind around. Why wouldn't any born again believer want to deepen their relationship with the Lord? It can only be because they have not yet seen Him in all His love, beauty, and grace.

When some Christians do not receive what they ask of

the Lord they become despondent very quickly. To them, prayer is getting their needs met, or receiving the manifestation to their desires. Any normal relationship becomes strained if all one person wants is material benefits. It is like a young boy who receives a much desired gift or toy from his father, but then he just spends all his time with the toy and never spends time with his father. That may be normal for a baby Christian or a young convert, but it is an infantile state of Christianity. We must move on from there and grow in our relationship with God. He wants us to enjoy His gifts and be thankful for them, no question about it, but we've got to graduate to a higher place of simply enjoying Him for who He is.

Fellowship is the reason God created man. Work on your fellowship and friendship with Jesus. Your faith will automatically work better then. Faith and love are twins. When you learn to love the Lord and fellowship with Him your faith works better. Faith works by love (Gal. 5:6). Don't trade your fellowship for a formula, or for anything else in life for that matter.

Lack of focus on the Lord will turn your fellowship into a formula – a mechanical something. Most people's lifestyles rule them to such an extent that they have no focus toward God. They live so much in the flesh and in the natural realm that they become a very soulish person who may even quote the Word, but they never learn to abide in the Lord. Sanctify the Lord in your heart (1 Pet. 3:15).

What does that mean? It means that you've got to cultivate an ability to see God in everything. Most Christians only see God in the good things, but not the bad. This greatly affects their fellowship. It's a compartment mentality.

In other words, believers recognize that God wants them to have a full, abundant, and prosperous life (John 10:10). When good things are not happening in their lives God is there, but in difficult moments, they can't see Him. It has to be the devil. The problem with that mentality is that it stops you from being able to see God in every circumstance. Most believers' ability to see God has to do with their environment and their circumstances, so their faith is very limited. We as believers have to grow past that.

Like every believer does, I've always rejoiced in the Lord when everything was calm and good. And I might rejoice in the Lord when things were not so good, but I used to do it from a heady knowledge because I knew I should. But it did not include an ability to see God in that difficult moment. I saw the kingdom of darkness and I saw the kingdom of light. It was almost as if God appears one day and then all hell breaks loose, and in my mind He wasn't there. It's me and the devil having a fist fight. The devil got in and I had to get him out. And in my thinking I had to break through that hell to find God again.

Then I started thinking differently in that God is

always present, and He doesn't change. Yes, life and circumstances change, but God is still omnipresent. God is still immutable. When your faith becomes developed to such an extent that you're able to recognize that God is here - He's always here, then you're going to start looking for Him even in difficult moments. When I say looking for Him in difficult moments, I'm not talking about looking for Him to get you out of difficult moments. Of course you don't expect difficult moments, but the Lord makes it very clear that we're going to have trials, and we're going to have hardships.

I don't expect difficult moments, but I'm not going to set myself up for false expectations to believe that the day is going to be absent from potential trials. I already have an understanding that I'm going to experience those things perhaps today, tomorrow, in a week, or a year from now. Those things are going to come my way, but the great news is that God is with me. Again, it's developing a moment by moment consciousness and awareness of God, and learning to abide in Him even in rough times.

Most believers are always looking for God to resolve their problems. And of course we want God to resolve our problems, but we've got to learn to love God even in the midst of our problems. I want to learn to enjoy God in the midst of my problems and difficult circumstances. When I enjoy God in my circumstances, the circumstances become different. They have a whole different flavor to them. They don't represent defeat any more. They don't represent fear any more.

This fresh perspective can help a lot of believers learn to abide in the Lord. Most Christians rightly believe that God is good and the devil is bad. So they fight the bad and believe for the good. But we never have any rest in the bad, do we? And the reason we don't have rest in the bad is because we really don't have the kind of faith that we need in the bad.

The faith that we really need to enjoy life is to see Him. That's the real faith, when we see Him. It's not so much what He does for us; that's good, that's great. Thank God He's forever taking care of us, but it goes beyond that. When I can see Him, when my faith is developed to see Him in all circumstances, then it brings me to a great place of rest.

And that resting place is the abiding place in God.

CHAPTER 8

ABIDING IN HIM

"I am the vine, you are the branches. He who abides in Me, and I in him, bears much fruit; for without Me you can do nothing" (John 15:5).

Jesus enjoyed unbroken fellowship with the heavenly Father. He left us with the Holy Spirit so we can enjoy the same quality of fellowship. Our lives will be marked with a deepening conformity to His image when we learn to enjoy daily communion with Him.

When an angel appeared to Cornelius in Acts 10 he told him that his prayers and giving had come up as a memorial before God. In other words, the memorial in Cornelius' life was the character of his heart. The memorial in your life is what you are doing inwardly toward God. What is the focus of your heart? The quality of your prayer life is determined by the focus and condition of your heart.

Most Christians find it very difficult to think of God outside of church services, church functions, and doctrines, or a few minutes in their prayer closet and devotional life. To say it another way, most believers do not have a God-focus in the totality of their lives. As I mentioned before, they have a compartmentalized mentality when it comes to their relationship with the Lord.

Often we are unable to think of God except in terms of assemblies, creeds, denominations, programs, campaigns, drives, preachers, and buildings, etc. These things, although useful, can often rob us of the true mind of the Lord and hinder us from cultivating the blessed life of unbroken communion with Him. It is so easy to become taken up with a thousand different things, even Christianity itself, while your personal fellowship with Him is forgotten.

On the other hand, it is possible for someone to pray 8 hours a day and still not experience much of God outside of their prayer closet. I know some people who pray less, but experience the Lord more in the totality of their daily life. Why is that? What makes the difference? It is simply because the entire motivation of their lives is loving Him whether they are doing "spiritual" work, or menial and mundane every day work, whether they are in their prayer closet, or work place. When you realize that your entire life is a contribution to the glory of God, you will start learning what it means to pray without ceasing.

"Rejoice always, pray without ceasing, in everything give thanks; for this is the will of God in Christ Jesus for you" (1 Thes. 5:17-18).

"And whatever you do in word or deed, do all in the

name of the Lord Jesus, giving thanks to God the Father through Him" (Col. 3:17).

"Therefore, whether you eat or drink, or whatever you do, do all to the glory of God" (1 Cor. 10:31).

Learning to abide in the Lord, becoming aware of Him every moment, and seeing Him in every part of our lives is the real key to an enhanced and enriched prayer life. It is a walk with God where you experience Him in every kind of environment, good and not so good. With most of us, when things are going well, we experience more of God, but when there are adverse circumstances and obstacles in our lives we don't experience as much of Him, or none of Him at all.

For example, you're driving to a very important meeting, and on the way you get a flat tire. It's real cold outside and you forgot your gloves, so you have a hard time changing that tire. You're frustrated because you're going to miss the meeting. You count your whole day ruined. You fight your emotions. You fight the devil. You're upset. This is where most of us live, isn't it? What's the problem? How do we get past that and still experience God in adverse circumstances?

Here's what it is for the guy with the flat tire. His focus is wrong. His focus was not God; it was getting to the meeting. If we're not careful, we step into an agenda or a list of things we've got to do, and that becomes our focus instead of Him.

Your environment changes when you focus on anything but Jesus. And it's not even so much that the environment itself changes, but you change in that environment. You walk into a store to purchase a few things, and someone you know sees you there and wants to talk to you. They want to share a testimony with you, or worse yet, spill all their troubles to you, or just chit-chat with you about life. But you have things you've got to get done, and this is the only day in the week you can do it, so you start getting frustrated, grieved, and by the time the conversation ends you are upset because you wasted so much time. The reason you are this way is because you are not able to see God in that moment.

A mind-set with an agenda as its focus usually winds up missing God in many aspects of life. We've got to learn to live moment by moment with one desire – not the desire of my agenda, not the desire of what I want, but one sole desire – to enjoy the Lord moment by moment and cultivate that.

So if you get a flat tire, or some person or circumstance interrupts your day's agenda you say: "God, you're with me, I've got everything, and I have no wants." And then often you find that God works everything out where your supposed delays become opportunities instead of disappointments.

Abiding in the Lord is best illustrated by the relationship between a caboose and a locomotive. The caboose is the end of the train and it cannot go anywhere without being attached to the locomotive. The focus of that caboose is just staying connected to the locomotive. The caboose is not trying to get anywhere. Its' entire purpose is only to stay attached. It has removed itself from its own efforts to get somewhere. It should be the same with us. We are not trying to get anywhere. We're enjoying Him in the now.

CHAPTER 9

PRAYER IN THE SPIRIT

A number of years ago I began to mentor a 43 year old man in my home town, whom my younger brother had led to the Lord. He also received the baptism with the Holy Spirit at that time. This man began praying in other tongues extensively from the very beginning of his conversion.

As this dear brother continued to pray in tongues regularly a new phenomenon started happening. He began uttering names in prayer that he didn't even know. This is the only way you could pray for all saints because you don't know all the saints. *"Praying always with all prayer and supplication in the Spirit, being watchful to this end with all perseverance and supplication for all saints..."* (Eph. 6:18). This is real prayer in the Spirit.

One day when I was a young student in Bible school a praying man named Phil Halverson was called up to the platform to pray. When he prayed it seemed like heaven opened and a spirit of prayer consumed everybody. I had never heard anyone pray with such unction and inspiration before. He would speak out names of people and places in prayer that he didn't even know. One time when he was just learning to pray this way it was reported that he was frequently uttering the words "Cookie" and "Candy".

Brother Halverson, wanting some assurance that he was on safe and scriptural grounds, spoke to the late Kenneth E. Hagin, a man of great spiritual stature, about this new phenomenon that was occurring in his prayer life. Rev. Hagin laughed because it turns out that those were the nicknames of his two granddaughters. Again, this is real prayer in the Spirit.

I remember also hearing a testimony of one of the pioneers of the Pentecostal movement in the early 1900's, before there was any organization among them. The only way they could communicate was in the Spirit. One day the Holy Spirit told this pioneer pastor to go over to another state and raise up a young pastor who was dying. That sounds a lot like Ananias being instructed by the Lord in the Spirit to go and minister to Saul. Specific details were given concerning Saul's exact location and condition, and calling (Acts 9:10-18). I'm afraid sometimes we can be so organized that we organize the Holy Spirit right out of our affairs and prayers. If you carefully examine the book of Acts you will find continual communication in the Spirit.

As we've discussed in this book, communication in the Spirit is real prayer. We know to pray for certain things the Bible instructs to pray for, but it would be impossible to pray for things we don't know about except it be in the Spirit. For instance, I know what to pray for concerning me and my life and family, but I don't always know about others. I think one of the greatest values of being baptized with the Spirit is the value of receiving our prayer language of tongues so that we are able to then pray for things we do not know about.

The apostle Paul speaks of two kinds of praying in 1 Cor. 14:14-15; praying with our spirits and praying with our understanding. Praying with our own understanding would be praying with our own minds and mental faculties. This is very limited praying because it is based on your own limited knowledge. But praying with our spirits is praying with God's understanding, which is unlimited knowledge. You see, all praying is not necessarily spiritual. Some of it is purely in the mental realm. For the most part, the Church has failed because it has endeavored to carry out the work of God only with mental praying.

"For we do not know what we should pray for as we ought, but the Spirit Himself makes intercession for us with groanings which cannot be uttered" (Rom. 8:26).

P.C. Nelson, a prominent Greek scholar, said that the end of v. 26 reads this way in the Greek: *"groanings which cannot be uttered in articulate speech (which is our regular kind of speech)."* This would include praying in tongues. Have you ever prayed and inspiration just wells up within you that you cannot express in mere words of your own understanding? That is the Holy Spirit helping you.

We don't know how to pray as we should sometimes. For example, we can pray for all those in authority as the Word instructs us (1 Tim. 2:1-2), but we don't know all that's facing them and what is happening behind the scenes many times. The Holy Spirit does, however, and He wants to help us pray into those areas. A prayer where you say, "God bless all those in authority" or "God bless so and so" is a bit shallow and inadequate. When you only pray mentally with your own understanding you often come to a wall where you know that your prayers are insufficient to bring forth the desired result.

At times you don't feel too much inspiration in prayer, but other times you feel like bursting. Usually it is somewhere in-between. We need to understand, though, that even when there's no inspiration, we can start out in faith and move into the Spirit by praying in other tongues. Thank God we don't have to wait around for a spirit of ecstasy to fill us before we can pray this way. It is difficult to explain the real value derived from praying in the Spirit or in other tongues to someone who has never experienced it.

The spiritual realm is not real to many Christians because we live so much of the time in the physical and mental realms. We make so much noise with our minds. Making a practice of praying in tongues and meditating on the Word will help our minds get quiet. It will take time, but you can get to the place where you learn the Spirit's touch, and you hear Him speaking to you by revelation or alerting you to something in prayer. The knowledge of certain things will just come into your spirit.

Prayer is like cooking or driving a car. You can't learn it unless you do it. You could study the driver's manual, but until you actually get behind the wheel, start the car and go, you won't learn to drive. You can read a good cook book, but until you get in the kitchen and start putting the ingredients together and cooking a meal, you won't learn how to cook.

Many talk of prayer, write about prayer, and read books on prayer, but until you pray you will not learn and grow in the art of prayer. In the beginning of this chapter I told you about the new convert in my home town whom I am mentoring. He was saved a short time ago, but is already praying supernaturally with tongues and at times interpretation. He has learned by doing it. He wouldn't have learned to pray this way if I had only taught him without him doing it.

It takes time to learn the Word and the Spirit in prayer. The prayer of faith (Mk. 11:23-24; Jam. 5:15) is the prayer most believers are familiar with. This is a prayer where you ask and believe and it's done. But those whom we consider to be people of faith and the Word make the mistake of trying to make this prayer work for everything and in every situation. By doing so we miss what the Holy Spirit is trying to teach us and do for us.

For example, if the Holy Spirit is alerting you to make intercession for somebody, praying the prayer of faith won't work. Now the prayer of faith will always work for you and your needs, but not necessarily for others. If it did always work for others you would never need to intercede for anybody. We must learn to be keen enough in the Spirit and knowledgeable enough in the Word to know what type of praying needs to be done in a situation. The prayer of faith and the prayer of intercession are two different kinds of praying.

Here's an illustration. One woman in a church kept getting this sense that something bad was about to happen to her son. Instead of praying and waiting on the Lord she didn't do anything. Not too long after sensing this, her son was seriously injured in a motorcycle accident and later died.

If this mother had begun to intercede and take hold of this situation with the Holy Spirit this tragedy might have been avoided. God was trying to alert her to pray. Then people question God and wonder why He allows bad things like this to happen, but He was trying to stop it.

Praying the prayer of faith in that situation would probably not have worked. Intercession was needed. The old Pentecostals knew something about praying this way. They called it "praying through". You've got to be keen in the Spirit and skilled in prayer to understand how and when to pray this way.

Sometimes you take hold with the Holy Spirit, but other times He will initiate a burden or reveal something to you and take hold with you. With things and situations you have knowledge of you can initiate and take hold with the Holy Spirit. But when it comes to things you have no knowledge of with your natural mind, as was the case with this mother, the Holy Spirit will reveal it and initiate a burden or a strong inward witness about it. Then He will begin to take hold with you while you cooperate with Him. This mother did not cooperate with what the Holy Spirit was showing her.

At the end of 2011, my 81 year old father had open heart surgery. It was not an easy surgery at his age and there were complications. I'm sure some of my friends were praying for him, but I was watching over him in the Spirit and talking to the Lord about it all the time. I didn't just pray the prayer of faith and call it done. It was a battle.

For example, I'd get a phone call in the middle of the night from the hospital and immediately my heart would sink thinking the worst might have happened, and perhaps we lost him. But I plead my case with the Lord and made a pact with Him, and I would constantly remind Him of it. And then I would pray in the Spirit and make intercession for my dad.

One night I prayed through and received a word from the Lord basically telling me that he'd be alright. Peace flooded my soul and from that point on that word became my anchor. In this case, if I had only prayed the prayer of faith once and claimed victory, things may not have turned out right. We must be sensitive to the Holy Spirit.

Many bad things that happen to people could be averted if they had been more sensitive to the Spirit of God and listened and prayed. The Lord Jesus Christ has given authority to His Church. That authority is carried out on the earth through faith and prayer. God is limited by our prayer life.

"It seems that God can do nothing for humanity unless somebody asks Him to do it." John Wesley

If you have a burden or a strong inward witness about something don't just rebuke the devil or speak a few words in tongues and claim the victory. God may be trying to alert you to something. Stop and wait on Him and see how the Holy Spirit will lead you and what He'll show you. If we take hold with Him He will take hold with us and win the victory.

CHAPTER 10

THE LOST ART OF TRAVAIL AND INTERCESSORY PRAYER

"My little children, of whom I am again in travail until Christ be formed in you" (Gal. 4:19 - ASV).

It is sad and painful for me to say this, but this younger generation knows very little to nothing about this kind of praying. I'm a little biased and in some ways spoiled, because I came up under the tutelage of one of the greatest men of prayer of this past century named Kenneth E. Hagin, also affectionately known as Dad Hagin. I've referred to him before in this book. I attended his Bible training center in the early 1980's when there was a depth of the move of the Spirit unlike anything we see in most circles today. Much of what I've written here today is from the wisdom I received from Dad Hagin and his life.

I am not given to a lot of travail and intercessory prayer in the same way my wife is. Over the years I've had moments of intensifying and agonizing prayer, and I recognize the Spirit of God in this kind of praying, but I don't live there like some of the old timers I've read about. The first time Dad Hagin travailed in prayer he didn't understand it, but he knew it was the Holy Spirit leading him. He had prayed this way before a service and had barely preached the introduction of his message when sinners made a run for the altar. He then realized what he had been doing before in prayer.

Do we understand the impact and the fruit that this kind of praying produces? It is immense! There is a place for church growth conferences and the training and tools that are provided at these conferences, but often prayer and the Holy Spirit are hardly ever mentioned. Without Holy Spirit-wrought prayer much of our labor can be in vain.

The Bible talks about travail but it also makes reference to groanings. Both of these elements of prayer are extensions of praying in other tongues. I would not feel safe in saying that one is greater than the other. I will say though, that one is more intense than the other.

"And in like manner the Spirit also helps our infirmities: for we know not how to pray as we ought; but the Spirit himself makes intercession for us with groanings which cannot be uttered; and he that searches the hearts knows what is the mind of the Spirit, because he makes intercession for the saints according to the will of God" (Rom. 8:26-27).

Groanings are a part of making spiritual intercession. Sometimes the yearnings in prayer that are inspired by the Holy Spirit are unspeakable and they come forth in groanings that are too deep to utter in common speech.

Concerning travail, this element is part of the same family and conjures up an image of a pregnant woman laboring to bring forth her child. This is the kind of praying these verses speak of. The apostle Paul travailed twice for the Galatian Christians – once for salvation and again for them to grow in Christ (Gal. 4:19). You can pray for sinners or for saints this way.

As much as I am a strong proponent of the Word, sometimes preaching and teaching the Word alone will not get the job done when it comes to salvation, or spiritual growth and transformation, or even healing. Some sinners will get saved just by hearing and believing the gospel. Others will not unless travail and spiritual intercession is made for them. And the reason many conversions or decisions for Christ don't amount to anything is because a confession was made or a prayer was recited, but there was no birth. Salvation is a supernatural birth. God doesn't want decisions but births.

The same truth applies to spiritual growth. Some Christians will grow from hearing the Word of God and being doers of it, but others will not until spiritual intercession and travail is made for them. Why is that? Because until Christ is formed in the new believer he will naturally continue to do things that are wrong and sinful even though he is born again. Ministers must teach new believers, but prayer and travail must also be made on their behalf. Paul must have taught the Galatians the Word of God, but notice he had to travail and labor for them in prayer in order for Christ to be formed in them, and for them to grow in grace.

This same principle of travailing for lost souls and for Christ to be formed in new believers applies to other areas as well. Very often before a church or ministry can come into fullness, spiritual travail and intercession have to be made to give birth to it. I've come to this place in my own ministry where I felt held back and knew that a new dimension of ministry needed to be birthed. Sometimes it requires help from others in prayer to bring it forth.

It's not just one man's prayers, but it's going to take help and perseverance from the body of Christ to give birth to what God wants to do on the earth. I heard Dad Hagin teach us that sometimes it's like there's a huge body of water above the USA, and if someone would pull a lever that water would come flowing down on us all. Saints, there's a body of blessing above us, but we must pray this way and give birth to it before God pours it out.

Many Christians talk about another big revival, a national awakening, a spiritual revolution, or another Jesus movement, but it's going to take more prayer, travail, and real spiritual intercession to give birth to it.

Will you enlist in this increasing army of pray-ers? Will you sacrifice even the legitimate pleasures of life to enter into this prayer life? Will you be a willing volunteer in the day of God's power?

Travail and spiritual intercession overpowers the works of the devil that hold people in bondage, very often against their own wills, where they find it difficult to make the right decision. This kind of praying works to the pulling down of strongholds. People need to be taught by precept and example of how to cooperate with the Holy Ghost in prayer.

For example, during altar calls where an invitation to receive Christ is given in evangelistic meetings or church services, many believers have an overwhelming feeling, but they don't understand what it is. They don't realize that it's a burden to pray for lost souls, and they don't know how to yield to it. We need to have more of this kind of praying so sinners can be truly saved. There's a difference between making a decision for Christ, following up someone who has made a decision, and being truly born from above by the power of the Holy Spirit. We need to pray this way privately for those in our lives who are not yet saved.

I've read stories and accounts of Charles Finney and his prayer partner Father Nash. Nash would go into a city usually with at least one other pray-er and they would rent a boarding room and spend a number of days in prayer and fasting before Finney would come and preach. They would groan and travail in deep intercession for a majority of that time. And here's the litmus test they would use to determine if the atmosphere was ready for Finney to come. They would look out the window, back in the days when many people were on the streets, and if anyone fell to their knees in conviction with an overwhelming sense of sin and God's reality, they'd call Finney to come. Have you ever heard of such a thing?

This is really how you possess a city. Evangelistic outreaches are fine. Doing personal work is fine. Following up on people is fine. But without this kind of praying these things fail and fall short. Yes, we have a great responsibility to preach the gospel, for we've been commissioned by Jesus to do so, but unless travail and intercessory prayer precedes it and succeeds it, the results and fruit of it are often minimal. But just as surely as a pregnant woman's travail will result in the birth of her baby so will spiritual travail and intercession result in giving birth to babes in Christ.

This is a lost art in the modern Church. Back in the 1980's there was a real move of prayer in this area, but pastors and churches backed off of it because people got weird and flaky with it. Well, the Lord wants to bring that back again because, frankly, there's very little hope without it. The world is in a desperate state of gross darkness.

Years ago the Spirit of God spoke these words to me under a strong unction:

"If My people will learn to pray and acknowledge Me as God I will bring conviction even upon whole cities. And some shall call it a phenomenon, but you will know it's

because you prayed."

I could tell you more old stories and accounts I've read of men of old that saw and experienced amazing things that have happened as a direct result of praying this way. I've witnessed a few of them myself. No, I have not seen an entire city fall to its knees in conviction, but I've seen a few unexplainable things that can only be attributed to spiritual intercession.

For instance, one day I was preaching on a street corner of a busy, noisy intersection in an African city. There were many taxis honking their horns and people on the sidewalks going to and fro buying and selling one thing or another. We had been praying every morning before going out to street preach, but on this particular day it was different. Suddenly in the middle of my preaching the entire area of this busy, noisy intersection became silent. You couldn't hear the cars or the people. It was strangely silent. You would've thought you were at a funeral. I recognized it as the spirit of the fear of the Lord. A great peace and calm filled the streets. I told the people about it and everyone stood motionless and attentive to every word I was preaching. Many were soundly impacted that day. Friends, these things don't just happen by coincidence or because of a sovereign move of God. Somebody prayed with some unction and help from the Spirit of God.

I realize that many saints are praying throughout the nations. Even in America believers are arising, but where is the revival in the Church and the awakening among the masses? I have to believe that it's coming. If just a few pockets of sincere believers across the globe take hold of this kind of praying and get after it, we could see a tremendous swelling of the influence of the Spirit of God. Sometimes you can sense a work in the Spirit that God wants to do, but He won't do it unless we carry it and pray it through. Birth must be given to it. More careless saints need to help carry that load.

CHAPTER 11

PRAYER AND FASTING

We were exhausted from traveling for nearly two days without much sleep. This was the first morning after our first night of real sleep during our first Israel tour.

Imagine waking up by the Sea of Galilee. That thought alone spiked a holy reverence in Carolyn and I as we began the day with prayer.

It was easy to pray. There was liberty. The spiritual air was light.

Our first thoughts were overlaid with the Spirit's thoughts. *"This was a happy place for Jesus."* Such a simple child-like thought, but we recognized its origin. This is where Jesus enjoyed great liberty.

In His home town of Nazareth they didn't receive Him. In the synagogue they stared Him down, and then almost ran Him down off a high precipice. When He set His face toward Jerusalem His mood changed. The liberty He enjoyed in Galilee was for the most part missing, and at best, short-lived in Jerusalem. Even Joseph and Mary, in their endeavor to protect baby Jesus, withdrew into Galilee when Herod's son began to reign in his stead. Imagine a principality who commands all male babies under the age of two to be killed. That was Jerusalem in the time of Jesus. But Galilee was a happy place for Jesus.

The Holy Spirit showed us the heart of Jesus in this place. This is where He began His ministry of power. The 40 day fast and wilderness temptations transitioned Jesus from being full of the Spirit to being full of power. There is a difference.

"Then Jesus, being filled with the Holy Spirit, returned from the Jordan and was led by the Spirit into the wilderness…" (Lk. 4:1).

"Then Jesus returned in the power of the Spirit to Galilee, and news of Him went out through all the surrounding region" (Lk. 4:14).

This is what's happening in some churches right now. There is a spiritual readiness to make advances through prayer and fasting. Many will begin the New Year this way, but the call for those who are watchful and hungry is to pray until.

Jesus knew that the liberty He and the disciples enjoyed would be temporarily gone during and after His persecution and death at Jerusalem. The disciples would be scattered until Pentecost when they would then go out in that same power.

Satan is an old devil and he kills liberty. It has always been that way. Jesus overcame first in the wilderness and then in the public arena. Like a skilled boxer, Jesus moved with quick jabs, hard uppercuts, and sweeping hooks and quickly put the devil on the ropes. Everywhere Satan went, Jesus had already been there. By the time He entered Jerusalem the damage to Satan's kingdom had already been done, and His fame had spread throughout all of Galilee and beyond.

We often forget that Jesus did not stop at the Jordan with the descending of the Spirit and the affirming voice of God the Father. He was led into the wilderness and opened up the region of Galilee to great power through prayer and fasting. Unlike Jesus, when we're often moved by His Spirit and sense His love, we stop and never go far enough or deep enough to loose cities and regions from long-standing strongholds built up by principalities and powers.

It's an important time now for the body of Christ to understand this vital truth about prayer and fasting.

While cruising in a boat with 40 other tourists on the Sea of Galilee my mind went to the battle Jesus fought for our redemption. We were on a cruise boat, but Jesus came on a battle ship. The Holy Spirit had just spoken to us about this the night before so it was fresh on my mind.

When Jesus started His ministry in Galilee He entered into it with a battle mind-set. He came on a holy mission. It commenced with 40 days and nights of prayer and fasting. He broke the region open with the power of God.

It gave me chills walking around the Sea of Galilee knowing Jesus based His ministry there. I thought about how the gospel of the kingdom He preached exploded with healings and miracles beyond Galilee and into Syria, Decapolis, Jerusalem, Judea, and beyond Jordan, multitudes followed Him (Mat. 4:23-25).

"Take up the whole armor of God" exhorts us to enter into the prayer life and reminds us of the battle (Eph. 6:10-18). The imagery is quite clear and intense. *"For we wrestle not against flesh and blood, but against principalities and powers…"* (v 12).

The Lord unveiled this truth that needs to be brought to our remembrance. He showed my wife and me that the reason some places are harder to break through than others is because Satan has set up his kingdom in these places with a long standing in it.

As an example, look at North Africa and the Middle East. These were places that once flourished with the gospel in spite of the opposition. The breakthroughs came from the prayer life of the Church that gave birth to the power. Once again today governments have established antichrist strongholds through the rule of Satan, making it more difficult to penetrate. **There's a greater responsibility before the Lord in those hard places to open it up for the salvation of the people who live there.** You are fighting for their eternal souls.

Jesus got victory over every strong man and every kind of demon force. He wants us to do the same.

"However, this kind does not go out except by prayer and fasting" (Mat. 17:21).

The key to a life of prayer and fasting is to continually stand and pray in that place of, "Not my will but Your will be done." That is the key to winning the battle. That is how Jesus won it.

If the disciples had not fallen asleep in the garden they would've been more ready for the battle. Jesus wanted them to get the victory in prayer and be able to understand that, and after a temporary setback, they did so later.

"Could you not watch with Me one hour" (Mat. 26:40)? Jesus asked Peter.

He wanted Peter and His disciples to watch and pray so that they would not enter into temptation. He wanted them to be sober-minded for He knew the enemy was as a roaring lion seeking whom he may devour. Jesus wanted His disciples to have this battle-ready mentality.

When we were missionaries in Gambia, West Africa it was a hard place spiritually - 96% of the population of this tiny nation were Muslim. In the prior years we had lived in Liberia and Sierra Leone where the gospel flourished among the multitudes. Everything came fairly easy. But in Gambia it was different.

The Holy Spirit reminded us of that battle where prayer and fasting became a priority, and where, by the Spirit, we dealt with the principality of that nation. We saw things change. A door that was closing was opened wider by God through prayer and fasting.

When we left Gambia we knew that if the team we trained did not stay in that place of watching, praying, and fasting, they would not continue.

This is where older men miss it in their ministries. They don't keep the same battle stance as when they started. The initial battle mentality they had evolves into a cruise mentality. It's easy to do.

When I went to Liberia as a young man I shaved my head and fasted for nearly the first 3 weeks there. I had an abundance of zeal for the battle, but years later, more feasting than fasting led to a cruise ship mentality.

It's time for the body of Christ to get out of the cruise ship and enter into the battle ship. There will be casualties, but we must stay, stand, and fight. The good fight of faith is a fight that we win.

Prayer and fasting positions us for victory and increases our chances 100-fold.

CHAPTER 12

WHAT CONSECRATED PRAYER CAN DO

There are a couple of reasons for the following testimony I am going to share concerning the beginnings of an outpouring that, at this writing, is still going on.

First of all, this is what true revivalists pray for, preach for, and live and die for. This is a real manifestation of what true prayer and consecration can birth. Secondly, I share it to encourage others to stir themselves up to pray.

Here is the report that just came in from a spiritual son of mine who lives in the southeast part of the United States. I'm not going to disclose his name or the name of his city or church because the Lord told him not to advertise it.

"We are preparing the house for anything to happen. We can't move most of the time. After 35 days of prayer the glory is almost sedating people. I dismiss the service, and people can't move for hours.

People are beginning to weep and go into travail on their jobs. It's amazing!

I'm getting calls of spontaneous laughter and drunkenness while walking into the doors of their homes and on their property. And people are repenting in deep weeping and brokenness without an altar call, or before I minister the Word!"

This is what consecrated prayer will do.

Put no confidence in the flesh or in the counsel of man, but put your total trust in God. Let's cooperate with the Holy Ghost and enter into the true prayer life. Meditate on this and stir yourself up to seek Him like never before. He wants to do so much more.

This is a tremendous example of what can happen when we mean business with God. Here is this one minister's testimony of how this outpouring came to be:

"I called for a time of prayer after the Holy Spirit arrested me at the end of last year and the Lord said:

'I'm calling you into a love affair. Will you come?'

I responded after weeping:

'Yes, Lord but I'm bringing a people with me.'

And then the Lord said:

'That's the response I was looking for!'

He also told me to make room for Him because He was coming in a way that I'd never experienced Him before. He told me to call His people into a sacred assembly and pray until.

On January 5th I called the church by example to nightly prayer. The more we prayed the more we desired prayer and transaction with the Holy Spirit.

The Lord also spoke to me that when I call for this time of prayer I should determine in my heart that if no one else comes, I should lead by example. He said that He honored Samuel when he would cry out alone on behalf of the people, and He would honor me.

He also said not to advertise this time of prayer assuring me that He would be my advertisement. So I told the people not to post it on Facebook or any social media.

People are beginning to come from various places and telling me that they felt they were supposed to stop by. A man came that had been diagnosed with bone cancer. While he was in the presence of the Lord he was healed. He returned to the doctor and there was no trace of cancer. Praise the Lord!

I've not mentioned this to many people, but the Lord has sent encampments of angelic hosts in the Spirit. I have seen and felt these ministering angels. I asked the Lord why so many. And He replied:

'They've been sent as a guard to my anointing that will increase gradually. I'm sending my glory in a measure so you can stand and be able to carry what I'm doing.'

When I asked Him how we can stand, He said to pray in

tongues (1 Cor. 14:2).

I'm only preaching what the Lord births while under this heavy glory. We are in the beginning of a move that I don't even want to belittle by calling it a revival. Bible belt revival concepts frustrate guys like us. We are crying out for a sovereign move and nothing else will work.

This move will be an apostolic movement that will be led by men who are moving in the Ephesians 4:11 mantle. This is a movement that will equip the saints with power and understanding."

THE MANIFESTATION OF OUR OBEDIENCE TO PRAYER

The following testimony of the manifestation of the glory of God is a direct result of obedience to focused and concentrated prayer.

"We wrapped up the day Sunday with the tremendous blessing of being in the presence of God for 9 hours. Just got home and it is 9:00 pm.

We didn't have any room this morning. I'm asking the Lord for direction and crying out for His timing. The Lord has directed me that He would be preparing a place that could host this outpouring.

There were people today that would be walking across the floor and get stopped still, unable to move. I know it's legitimate because it happened to me on Saturday night. I was instantly glued to one spot and couldn't move for an hour and a half. I would laugh and then weep.

We will not stop praying until the heavens are opened and the Lord moves in. Please pray for provision. I know it's not about a building, but people are beginning to come from other places. We have a small place full of the glory of God. I will not go anywhere unless the Lord goes with us.

The Lord gave me a word of knowledge this morning about a left leg full of infection from a deep wound. I spoke it forth and instantly the fire of God hit a visitor, and he raised his hand and responded, "That's me! How did you know?"

I didn't explain it to him, but just commanded him to be healed in Jesus' name.

A shoulder injury was also instantly healed in the Lord's presence. Many others are being healed while in His presence. The Lord is moving, but He wants to move in an even greater manner.

We are asking the Lord for provision because we're having parking problems and other tenants are complaining. It's a good problem but I'm burdened.

A lady who lives an hour away testified today that when she got in her car to come here this morning she began to shake profusely and her husband couldn't stop weeping. She wept and was given her new prayer language today.

While doing a baby dedication this morning I saw in a vision a left eye that was almost blind. I spoke it out and a lady began to weep and was instantly healed.

People are weeping on their way to church while in transit.

I've already begun to hear that the Lord will prepare the team. I'm already seeing people grow weary from nightly prayer. I'm having to pastor and give people nights off to get rest. I'm down to a small remnant of people praying, but I would rather die than not be in this outpouring. I will not relent until the Lord fulfills what He promised He would do if we pray.

I'm not going to reveal this thing until the Lord gives me the go ahead. I'm afraid of quenching the Spirit. He said He would advertise. I'm desperate with a deep yearning within, and words can't express the way I feel. I'm sleeping very little and waking up with travail. The Lion of Judah is on the move! He's roaring in my heart and I'm overwhelmed by His hunger.

I got a call to minister in a place where we had revival last year. They asked me to return, but I told them I couldn't because I was committing my life to prayer. I told them perhaps I would come next month.

While we're texting, people are texting me and telling me

they can't stop shaking and weeping in their homes. We are in the beginning stages of the outpouring the Lord promised."

These same type of results and manifestations of God's presence and power are ours if we will pray effectually and fervently.

I close this book now with an inspiring quote from Kenneth E. Hagin on prayer that I've never forgotten.

"If we can just teach a few people to really pray, we can change the course of nations."

Concluding Note: I believe with all my heart that God's pattern has always been to invade and take His eternal place in the heart and soul of man, and from there reveal Himself to the world (John 17:23) (Col. 1:19, 2:9-10). The outward work of man will always impress us if we have not seen the mighty work of God done within us. It is within He takes His place and then reveals His work (John 14:10-12).

Allowing God to take His eternal place in our hearts and being baptized in the Holy Spirit with the initial evidence of speaking in new tongues is the beginning of a fruitful life of prayer.

ABOUT THE AUTHOR

Bert M. Farias is an author and revivalist who ministers in various camps across the body of Christ, both interdenominationally and cross-culturally. He carries a spirit of revival with an emphasis on holiness and the Holy Spirit with the goal to make disciples. He's ministered in Bible schools, churches, conferences, crusades, homes, small groups, and on the streets both in America and overseas.

OTHER BOOKS BY
BERT M. FARIAS

MY SON, MY SON

SOULISH LEADERSHIP

PURITY OF HEART

THE JOURNAL OF A JOURNEY TO HIS
HOLINESS

THE REAL GOSPEL

THE REAL SPIRIT OF REVIVAL

THE REAL SALVATION

To order any of these books, visit our website or
Amazon.com.

To become a monthly partner with Holy Fire Ministries, schedule a speaking engagement with Bert and/or Carolyn, or to receive the ministry's free newsletter please contact:

HOLY FIRE MINISTRIES

PO Box 4527

Windham, NH 03087

Website: www.holy-fire.org

Email: adm@holy-fire.org

24894260R00045